AF480172

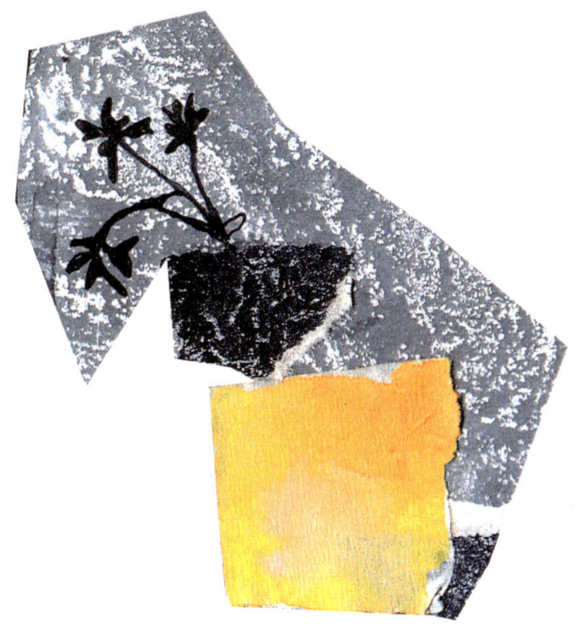

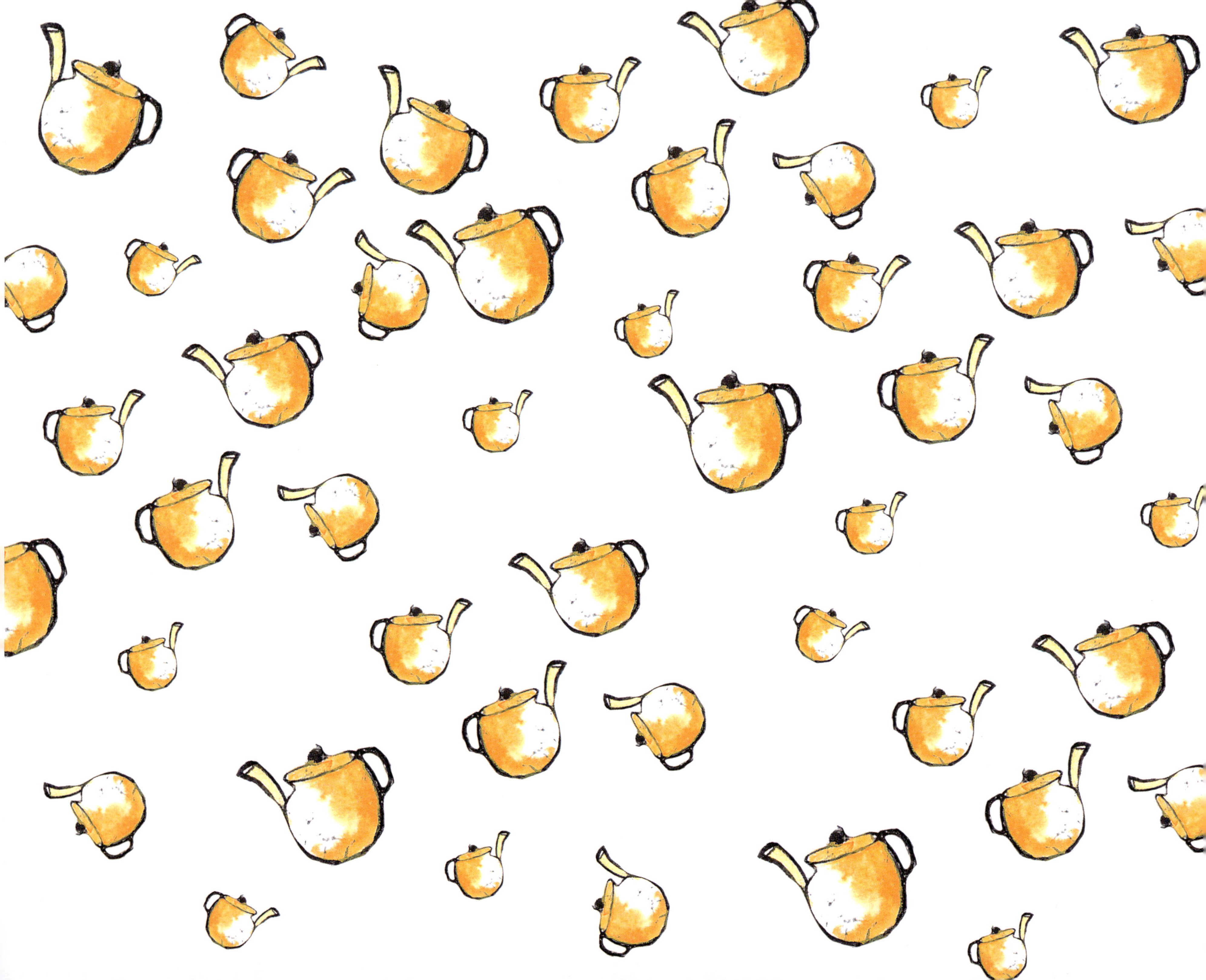

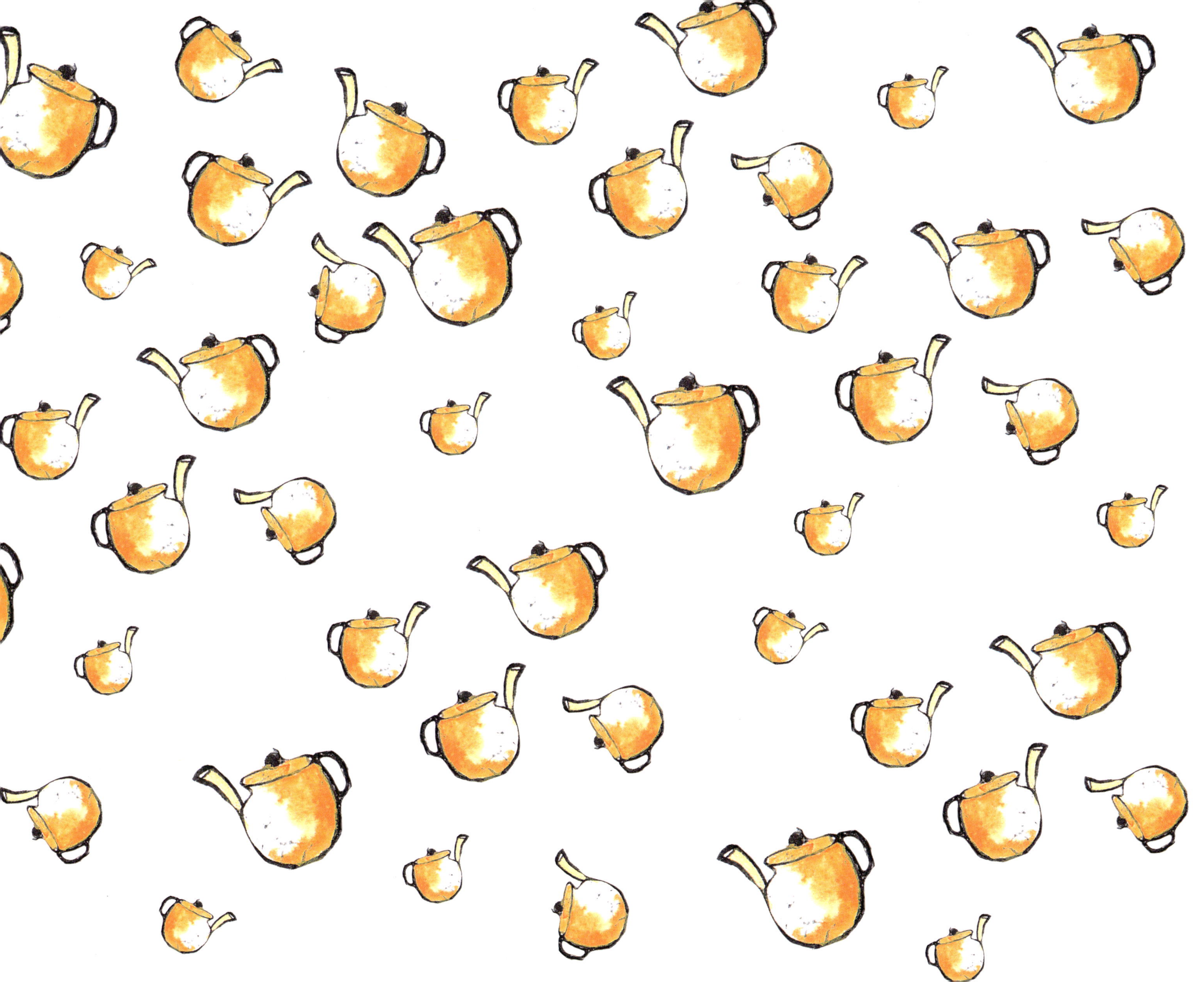

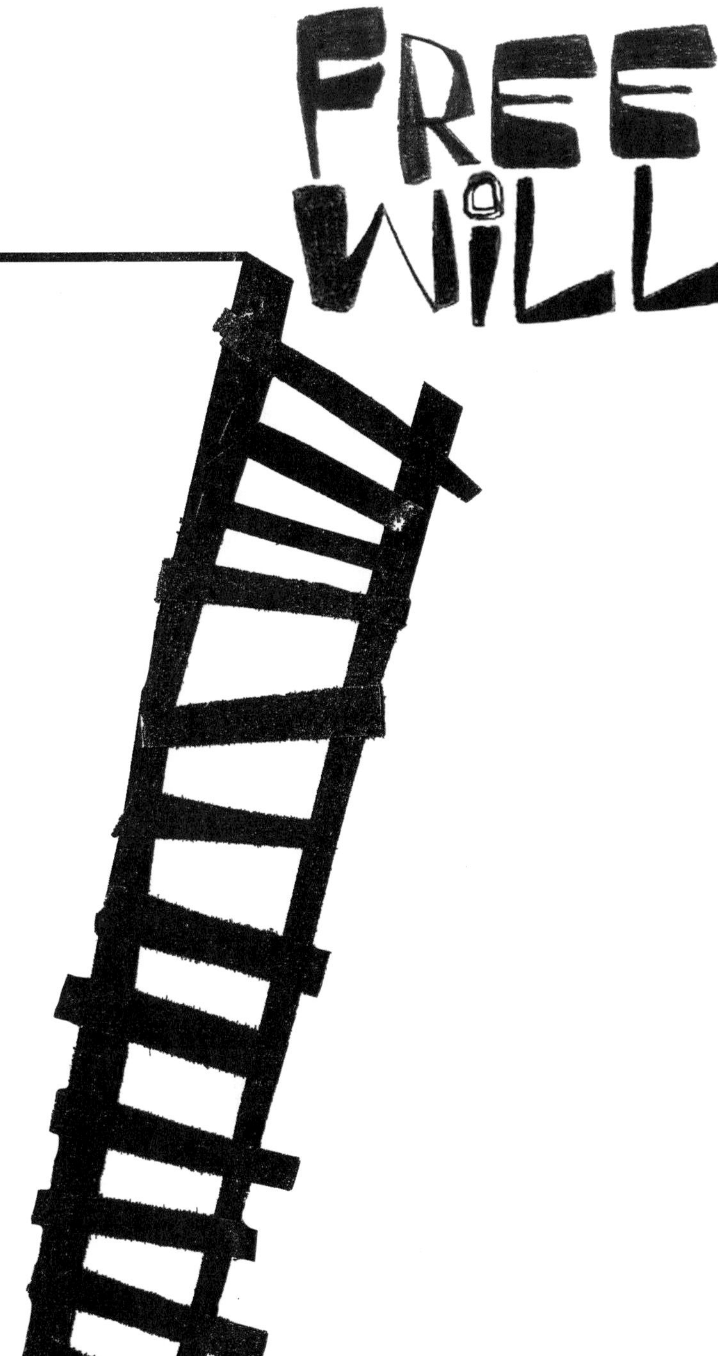

FREE WILL
BAHAR TAGHIANI

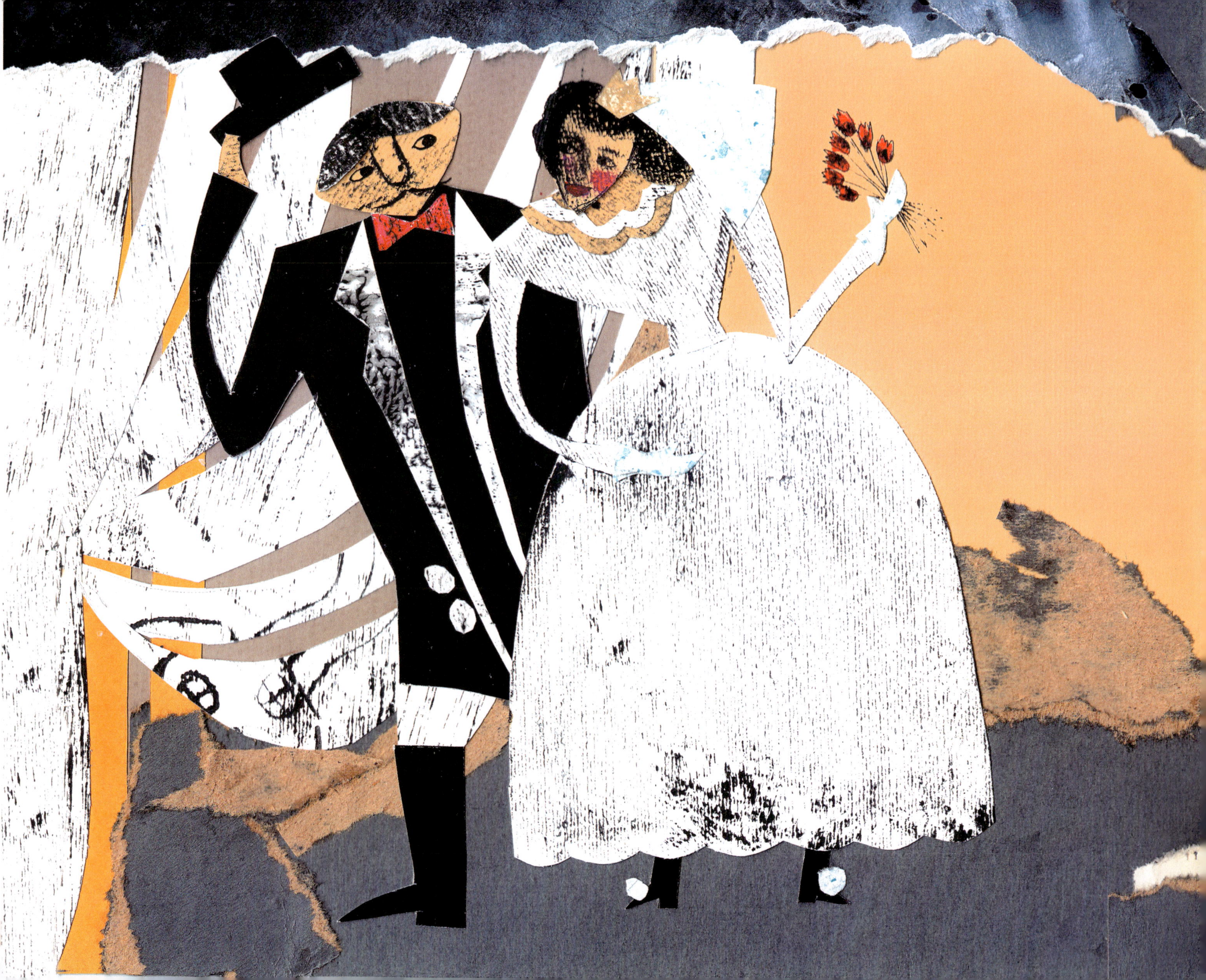

THE GIRL IS MARRIED.

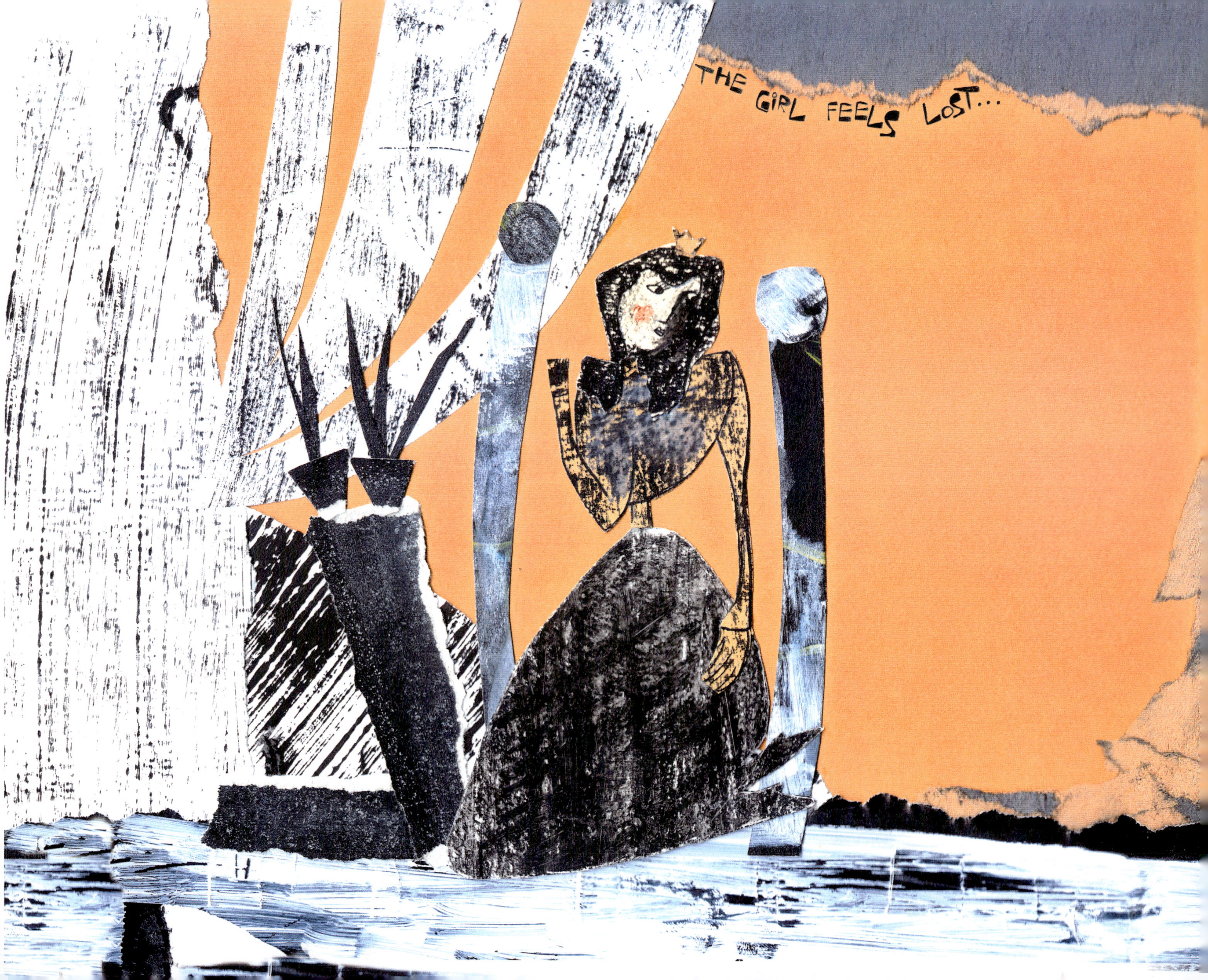
THE GIRL FEELS LOST...

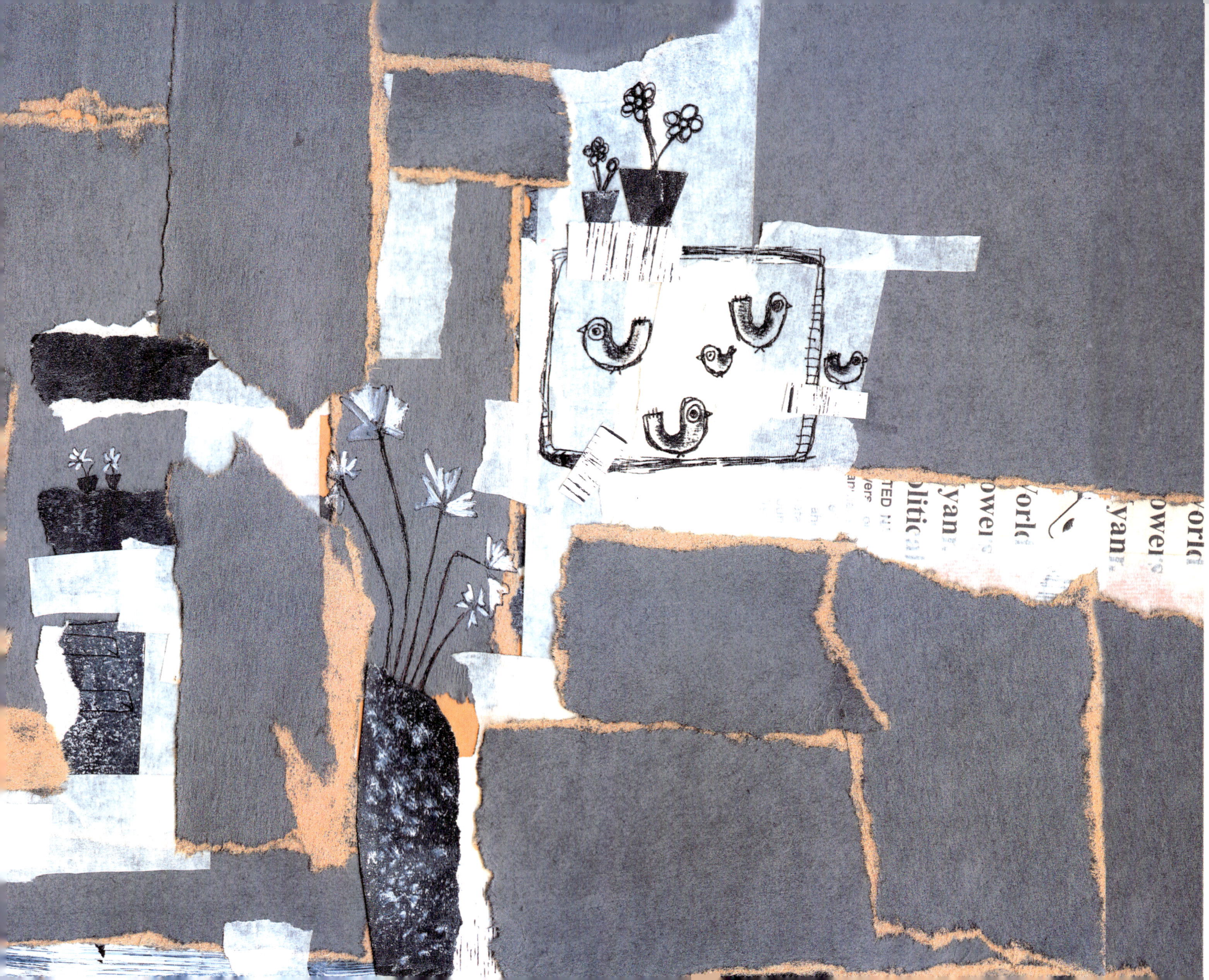

World
owel
yan
olitic
orld
owel
yan
TED N

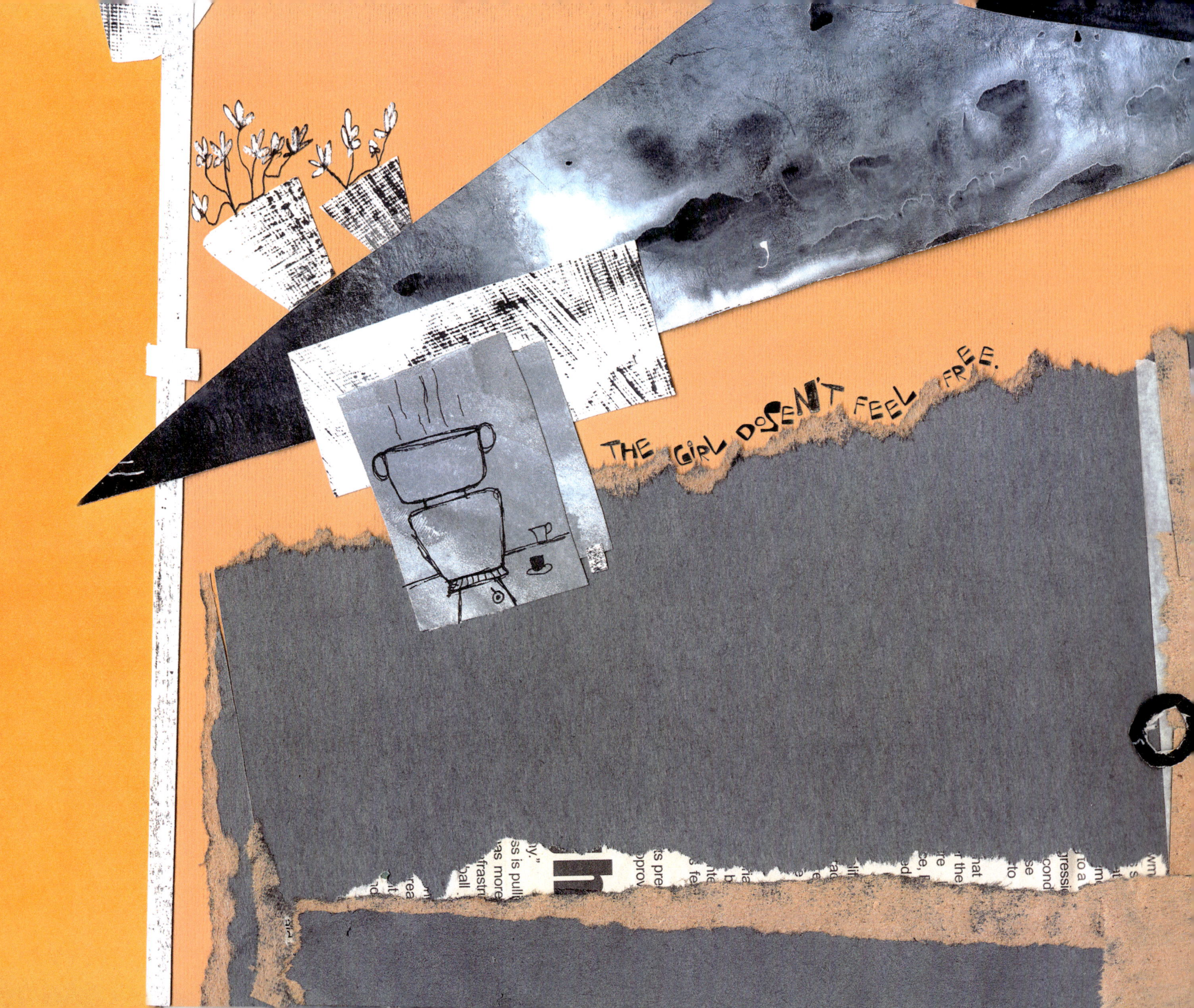

THE GIRL DOSEN'T FEEL FREE.

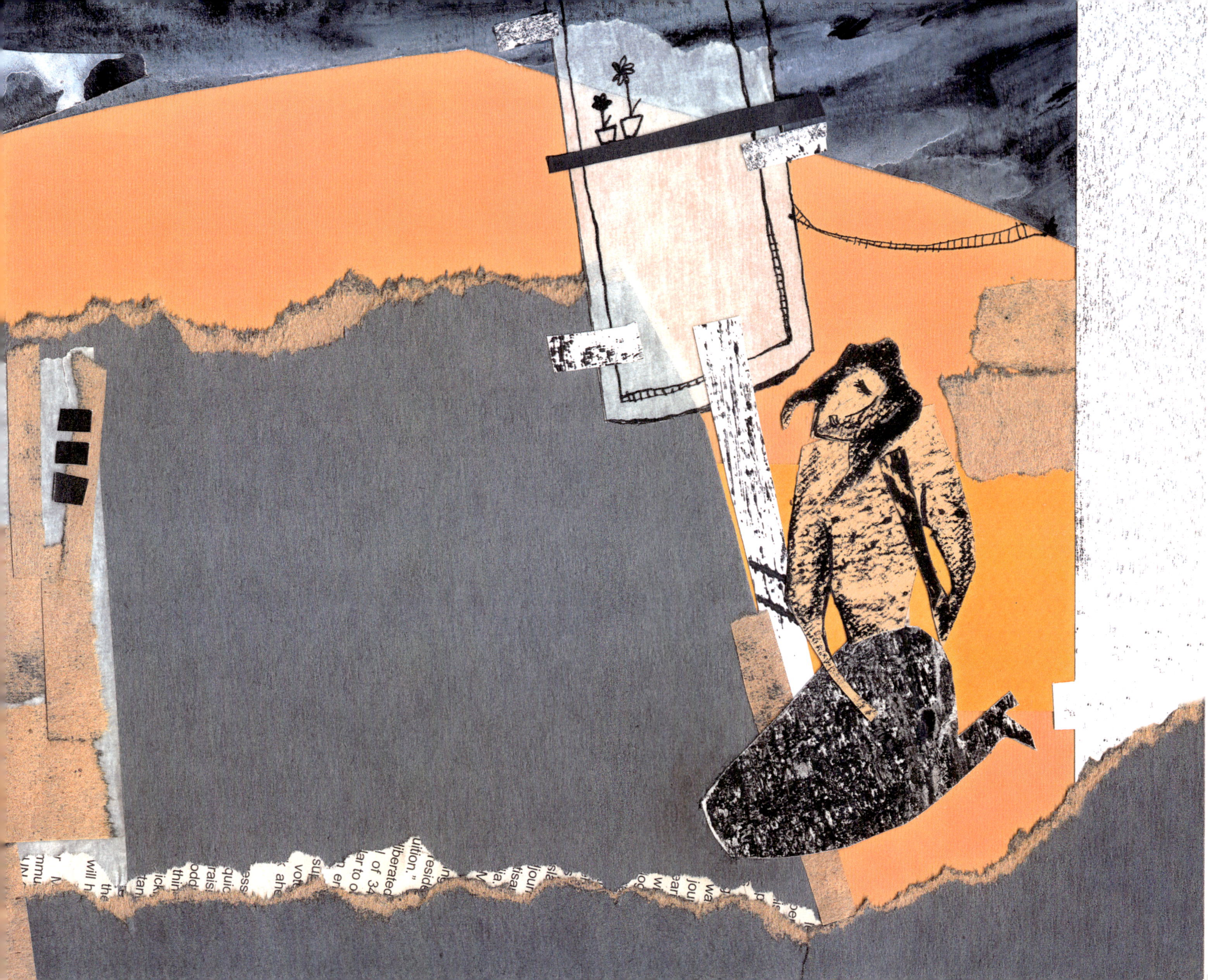

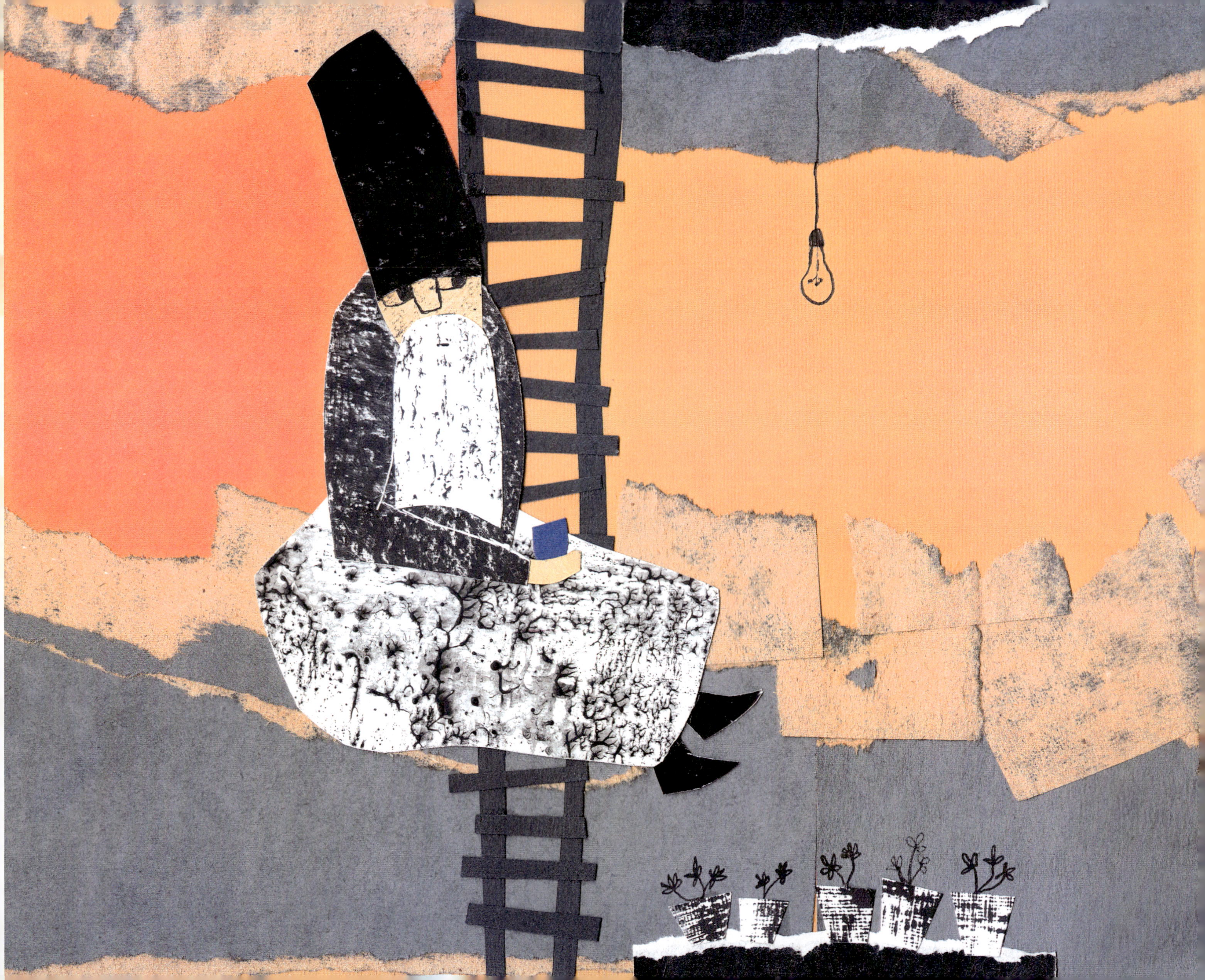

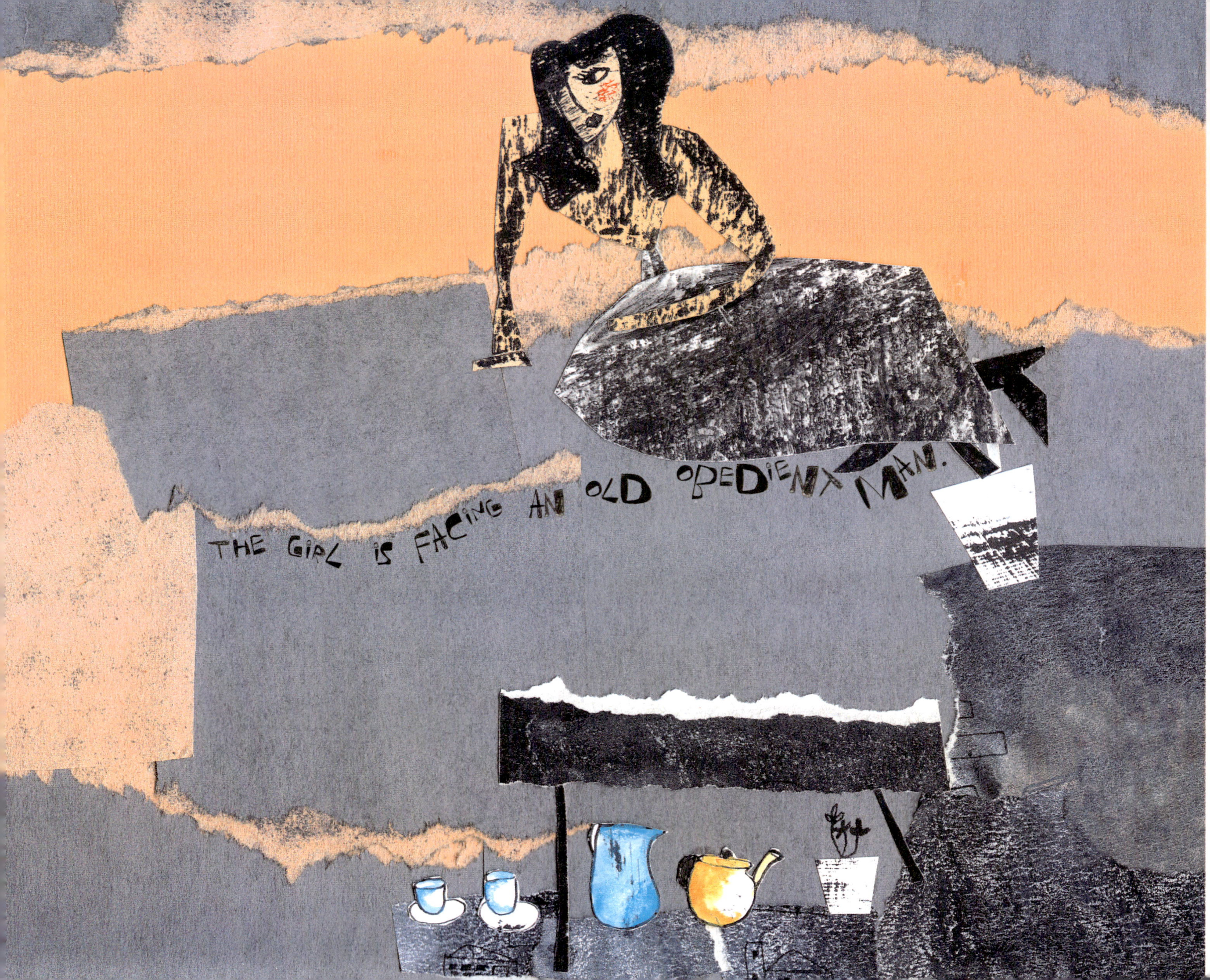

THE GIRL IS FACING AN OLD OBEDIENT MAN.

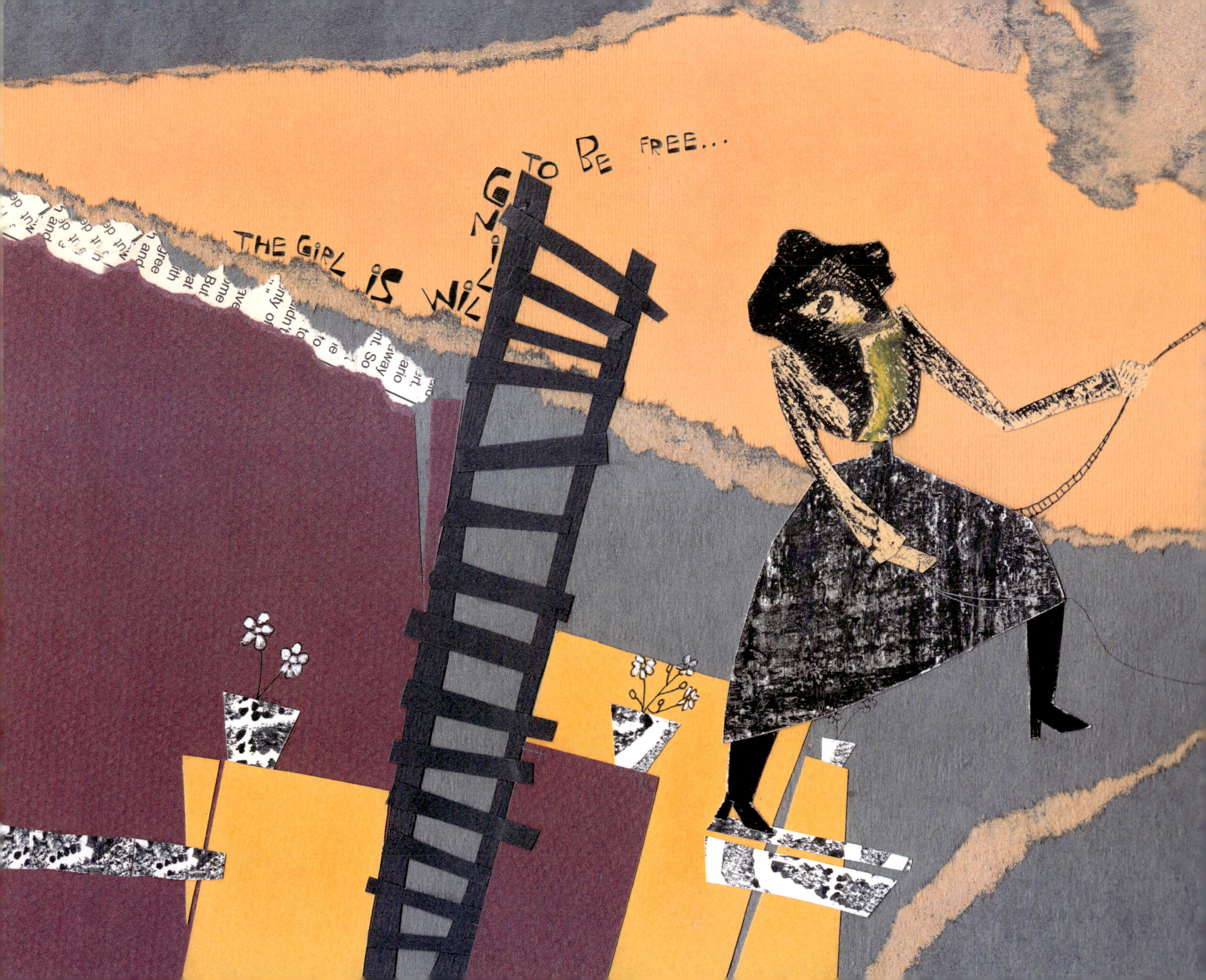

THE GiRL IS WIL...NG TO BE FREE...

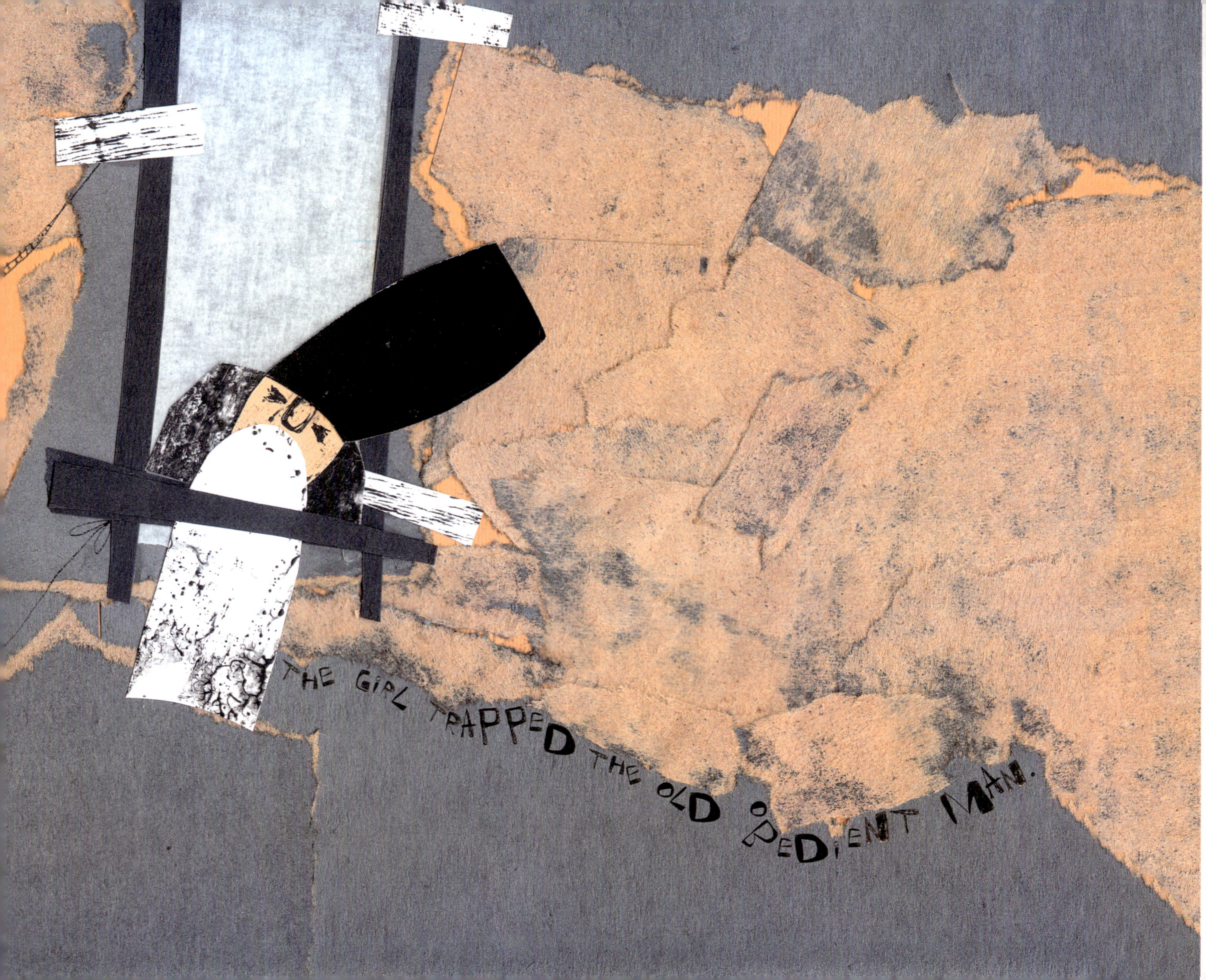

THE GIRL TRAPPED THE OLD OBEDIENT MAN.

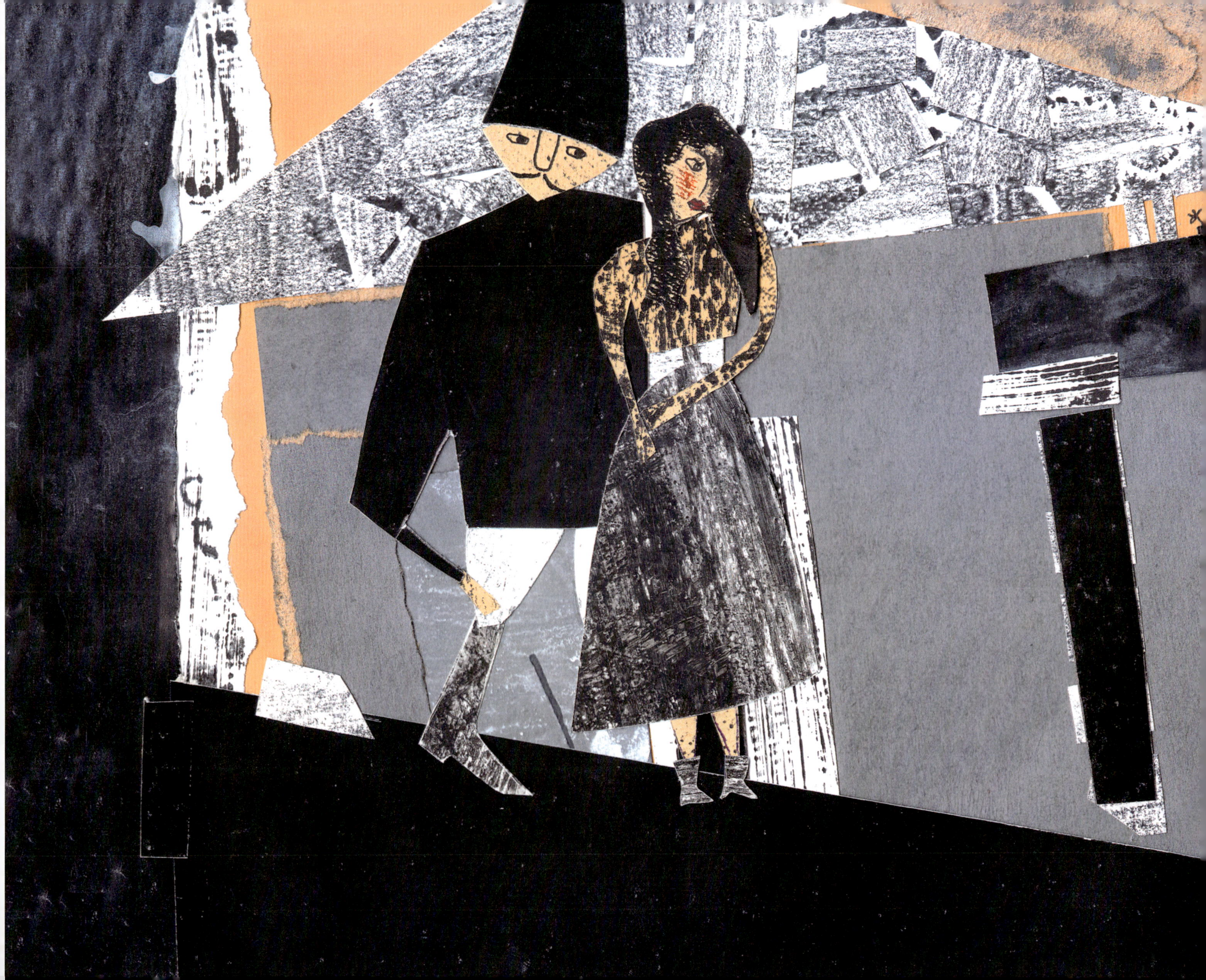

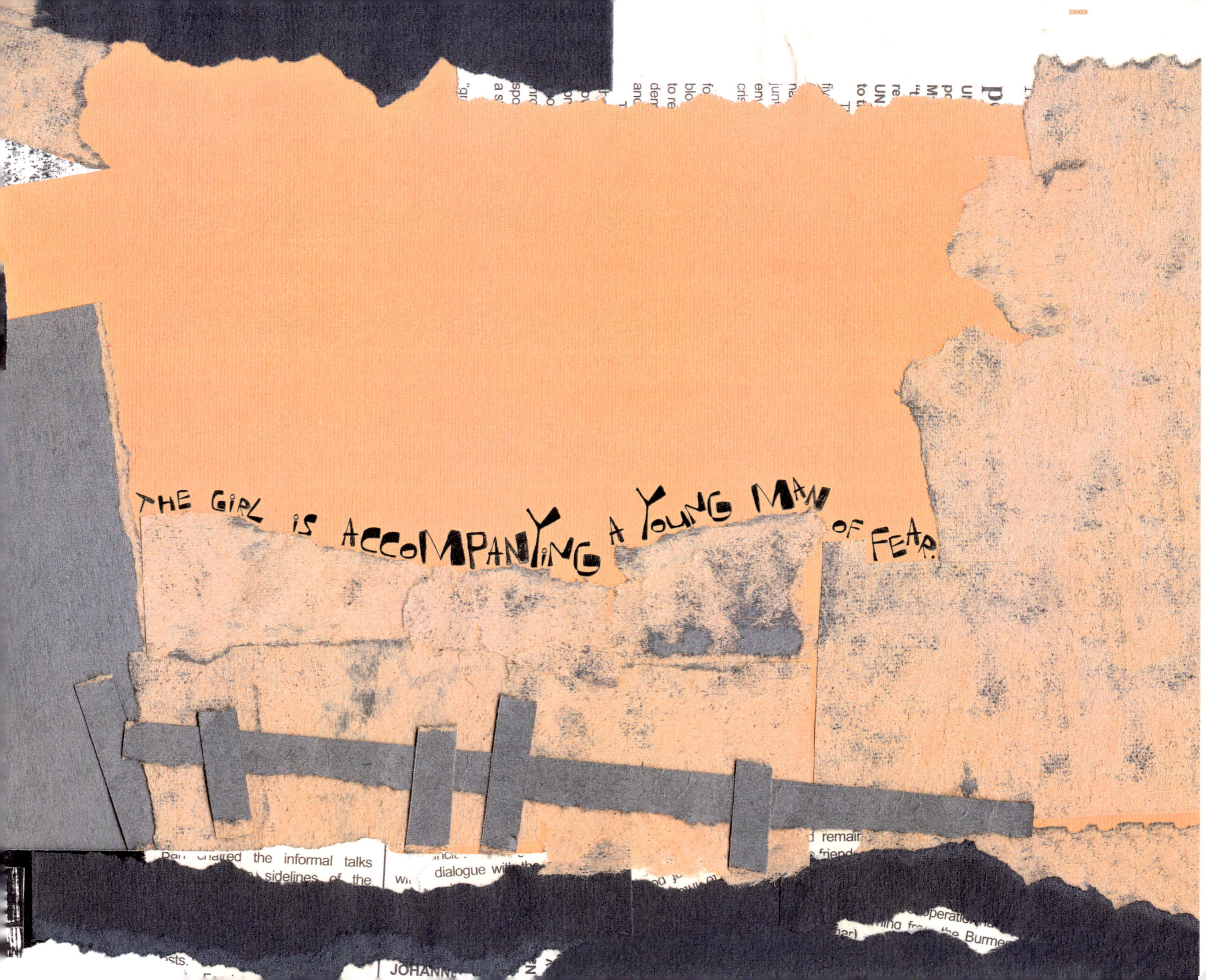

THE GIRL IS ACCOMPANYING A YOUNG MAN OF FEAR.

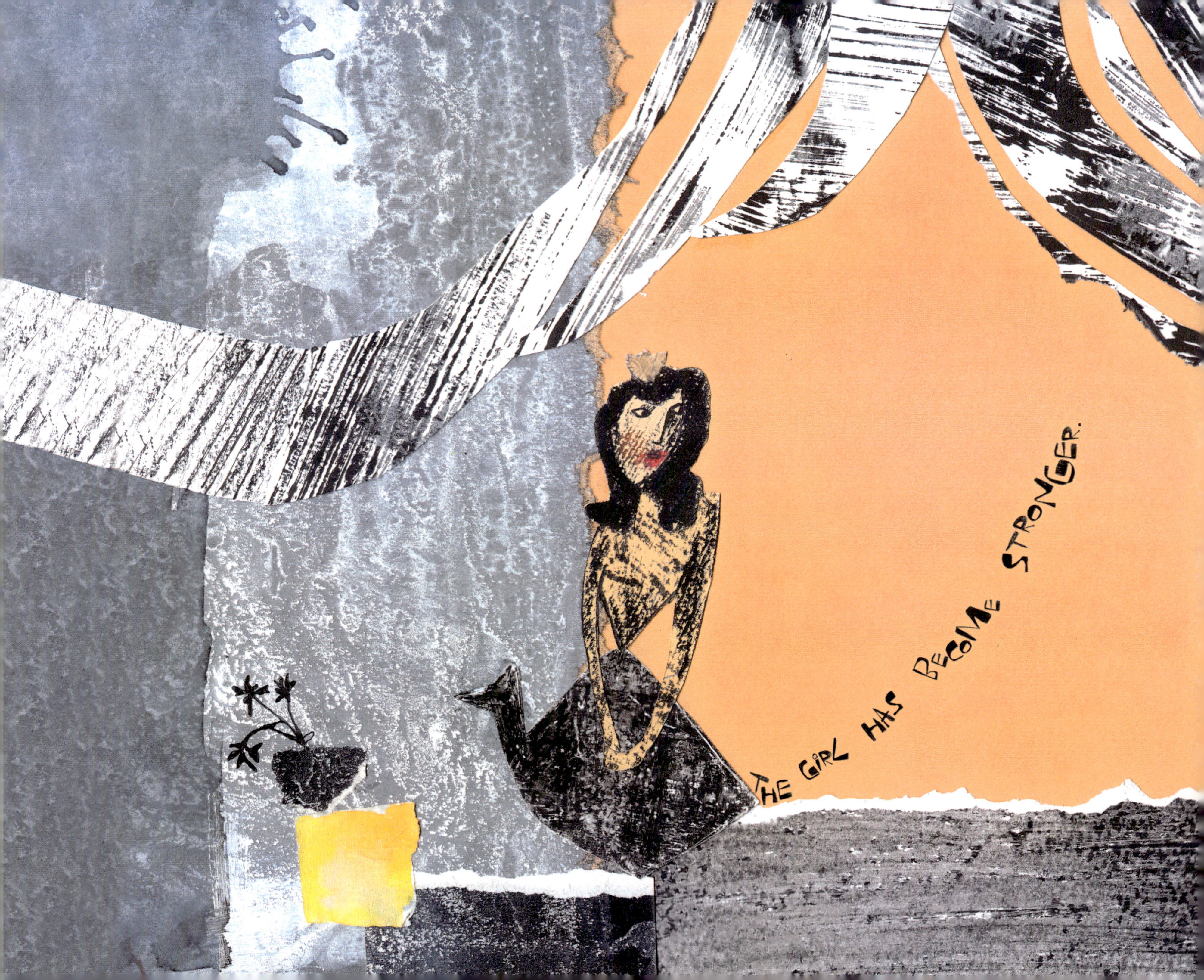

THE GIRL HAS BECOME STRONGER.

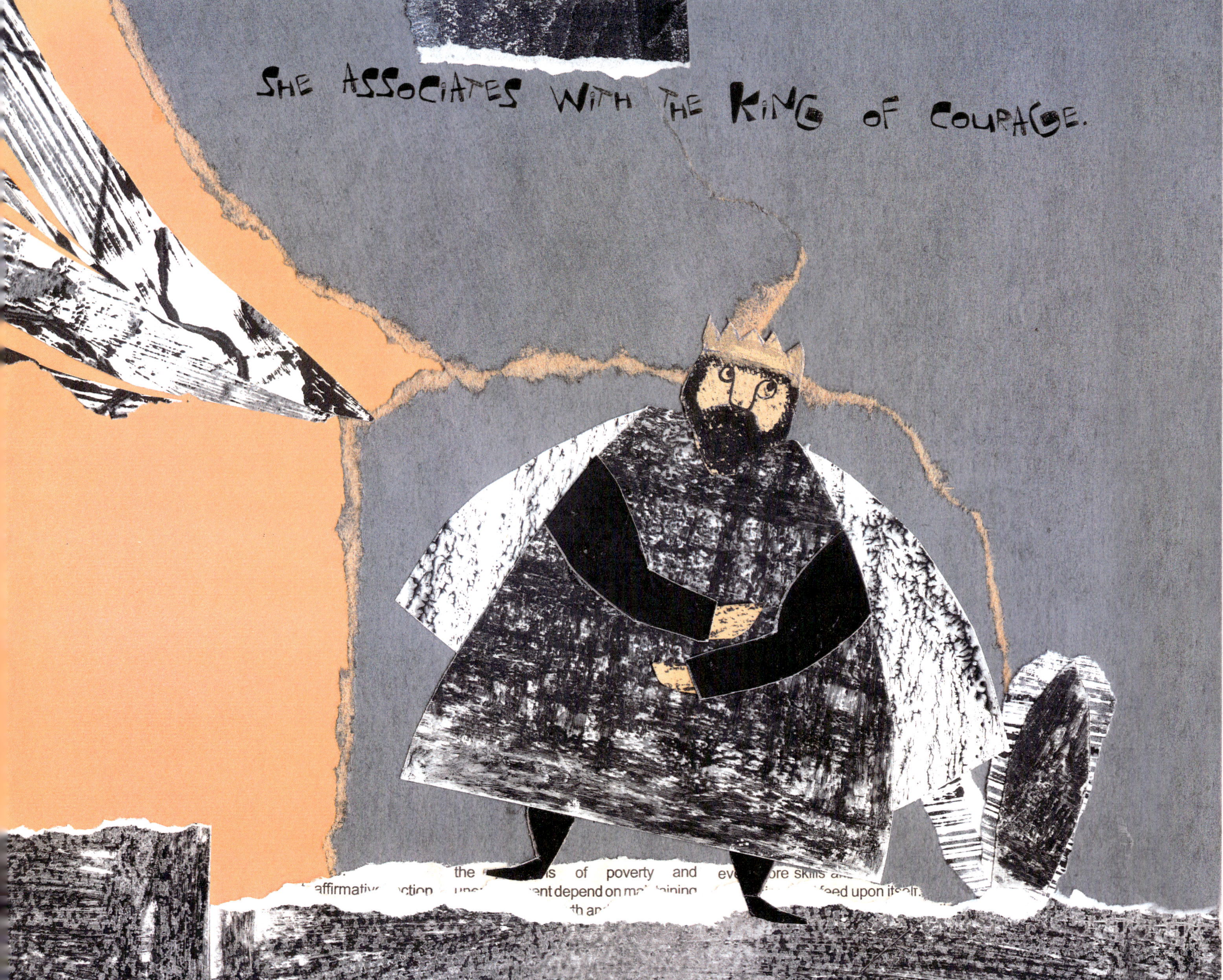

SHE ASSOCIATES WITH THE KING OF COURAGE.

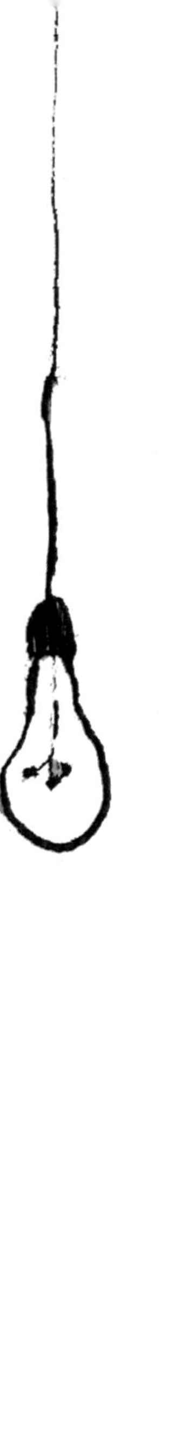

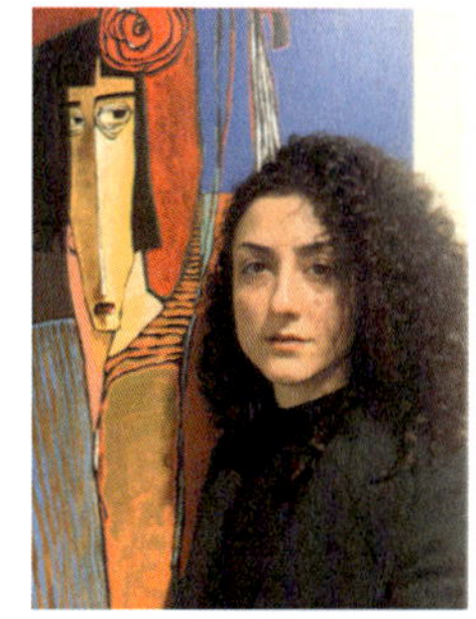

Bahar Taghiani is an illustrator and visual artist whose love for visual imagery began in early childhood. She started by creating characters out of pieces of paper, placing them in imagined stories, and bringing them to life. Today, her artworks are primarily created using mediums such as acrylic, collage, colored pencil, and watercolor, drawing inspiration from her perception of the world around her. Bahar is an award-winning artist, recognized by UNICEF for her illustration in the competition "Children on the Eve of New Year."

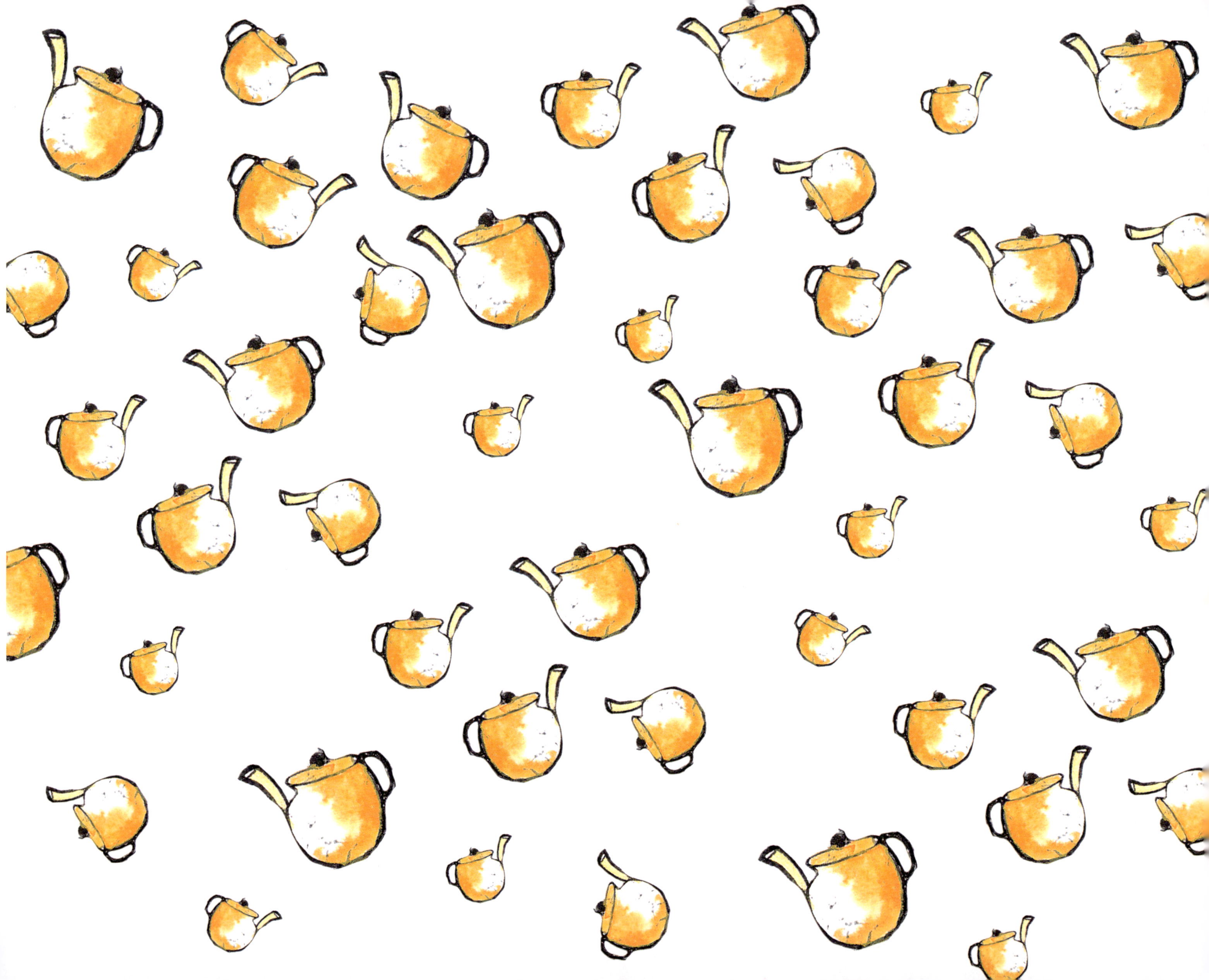

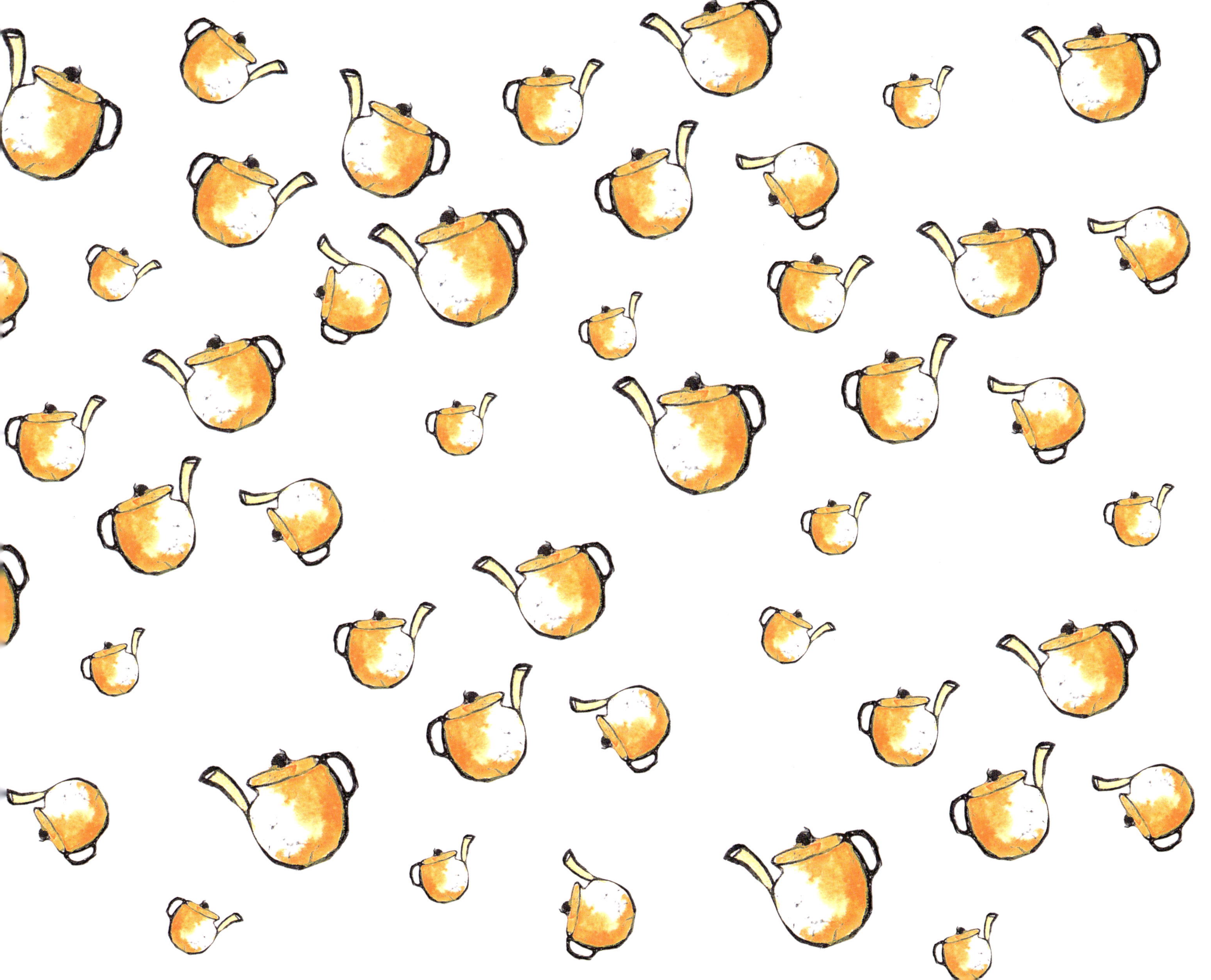

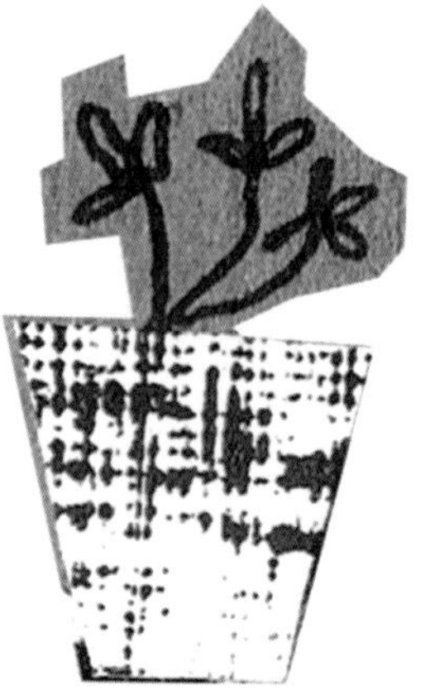